The Wampanoag

Stacy DeKeyser

Franklin Watts
A Division of Scholastic Inc.
New York • Toronto • London • Auckland • Sydney
Mexico City • New Delhi • Hong Kong
Danbury, Connecticut

For my parents, Nick and Doris Chaconas

Note to readers: Definitions for words in **bold** can be found in the Glossary at the back of this book.

Photographs © 2005: Bridgeman Art Library International Ltd., London/New York: 19 (New York Historical Society); Brown Brothers: 41; Corbis Images: 22 (Bettmann), 42 (Lee Snider), 24 (Joseph Sohm), 8 (Chase Swift), 28; Getty Images/Kean Collection: 9; Hulton|Archive/Getty Images: 36; Nativestock.com/Marilynn "Angel" Wynn: 7 (Francis Compte), 3 left, 4, 5, 6, 44, 46, 47, 48, 50; North Wind Picture Archives: 35 (Howard Pyle), 10, 14, 16, 27, 32; Stock Montage, Inc.: 3 right, 12, 18, 21, 39.

Cover illustration by Gary Overacre

Map by XNR Productions Inc.

Library of Congress Cataloging-in-Publication Data

DeKeyser, Stacy.
 The Wampanoag / by Stacy DeKeyser.
   p. cm. — (Watts library)
 Includes bibliographical references and index.
 ISBN 0-531-12298-0 (lib. bdg.)
 1. Wampanoag Indians—History—Juvenile literature. 2. Wampanoag Indians—Social life and customs—Juvenile literature. I. Title. II. Series.
E99.W2D45 2005
974.4004'97348—dc22

2004024310

Contents

The Wampanoag have lived on the east coast of New England for hundreds of years.

Chapter One

"People of the First Light"

The Wampanoag are an American Indian people of southern New England. Their ancestral home included what is now southeastern Massachusetts and eastern Rhode Island, from Narragansett Bay to the tip of Cape Cod, and the islands of Martha's Vineyard and Nantucket.

Origin of the Name

Wampanoag means "People of the First Light." They lived on the easternmost edge of the land, and were the first to see the sun rise every day.

The Wampanoag are best known for two very different contributions to the early European settlement of North America. First, they were the compassionate, generous people who helped New England's first white settlers to survive. Then, barely fifty years later, they battled against those settlers in one of the most deadly wars ever fought on American soil.

An Ancient Culture

The Wampanoag thrived in their lands for perhaps five thousand years before Europeans arrived. They built dwellings called **wetus**, or wigwams, by sinking long thin wooden poles into the ground in a circle. The poles were bent toward the center and tied together. Then the poles were covered with

This is a modern recreation of a traditional wetu. This wetu uses bark as its covering.

Part of the year, the Wampanoag lived by the ocean.

mats of woven grass, leaving a hole at the top for smoke to escape. In the winter, the poles were covered with animal skins for extra warmth.

The Wampanoag had a well-established system of planting, hunting, and fishing. During the spring and summer, they lived in seaside or riverside villages, where the men would fish with large nets. Each family had its own wetu. Women and children cleared plots of land and tended fields of corn, beans, and squash. In the autumn, after the harvest, the Wampanoag village celebrated. They feasted, danced, and said prayers of thanks to Kiehtan, the creator spirit.

Corn was central to the Wampanoag diet. It was so important that they considered it a sacred gift from Kiehtan. They even considered corn to be vital for life after death, and often included a supply of corn in a person's grave.

An All-American Food

Corn (or maize) is native to the Americas. It was first cultivated by American Indians in Mexico and South America more than seven thousand years ago.

During the winter, the Wampanoag relied on the animals they could hunt, such as deer, and on corn crops that had been dried for their survival.

During the winter months, the entire village moved to a sheltered spot farther inland. There, they built larger, oval-shaped wetus where several families could live together. During the cold months, they ate supplies of dried corn. The men of the village hunted for deer and fowl, often traveling many miles on foot in the bitter cold.

Government and Religion

Wampanoag government was based on community leaders called **sachems**. A sachem could be male or female, but was usually a man who inherited the position from his mother or father. However, a sachem needed to demonstrate wisdom and leadership in order to earn the respect of his community and keep his position. He rarely made decisions on his own, but was expected to consult a council of advisors.

Each Wampanoag community had a leader called a sachem. This position was often passed down from generation to generation.

One of the sachem's advisors was the **powwaw**, or holy person. The powwaw was a person with special powers who conducted rituals of prayer, cleansing, and healing.

Religion was a part of daily life for the Wampanoag. They believed that the world was full of spirits who provided them with food, protected them from illness, and punished them for wrongdoings. Every creature and object was a gift from the spirits and was treated with respect.

This respect for all things is the basis for the Wampanoag practice of **reciprocity**. Reciprocity means equal giving and

A Familiar Word

Because many healing or praying ceremonies were held in front of the entire community, any cere- monial gathering of American Indians eventually came to be known as a powwaw.

The Wampanoag believed that it was important to share what they received from nature, such as corn.

receiving. Nature gave freely of itself by providing fish, deer, and corn. The Wampanoag, in turn, were expected to share freely with others. In this way, the sick and elderly in the community were always cared for. Visitors were always given food and a bed. Any gift or favor would eventually be repaid.

An injustice had to be repaid as well. Therefore, clashes were common between the Wampanoag and neighboring tribes. These wars were usually small and isolated, involving only a few members of each tribe. Young men who proved themselves in battle gained respect and social standing among their people.

Territorial Boundaries

Many such battles were fought over territory. The Wampanoag, like other Indian peoples, believed that no one could own the land. However, they could claim certain territory for the **exclusive** use of their tribe. Such land claims were necessary to ensure that each tribe had enough land to provide for fishing, planting, and especially for hunting.

The Wampanoag's neighbors included the Nipmuc, Massachusett, Abenaki, and Narragansett. These groups were all loosely related. They shared common ancestors and spoke similar languages. Despite their similarities, each group had a separate identity and territory. For the most part, the groups lived in peace. The Narragansett, however, were always troublesome. They were the largest and most powerful tribe of southern New England. Located across the bay to the west of Wampanoag lands, the Narragansett frequently challenged the territorial boundaries of the Wampanoag.

Still, the Wampanoag managed to defend their lands. For hundreds of years, a balance of power and territory was maintained among all the tribes of southern New England. Then, an invisible enemy from across the sea began its attack in the 1500s. This enemy was disease. It was the first of several forces from Europe that would change life for the Wampanoag forever.

Giovanni da Verrazano was one of the first Europeans that the Wampanoag encountered.

Chapter Two

When Strangers Came

In 1524, an Italian explorer named Giovanni da Verrazano sailed along the coast of what we call New England, looking for a passage to Asia. He and his men went ashore, where they met members of the Narragansett and Wampanoag nations.

In the years to follow, other Europeans came and went more frequently.

They sailed from France, England, Sweden, and the Netherlands. Some were fishermen, who knew that cod were plentiful in the cold north Atlantic waters. Some were explorers, looking for a shortcut to Asia. Some were traders who were looking for exotic items, such as beaver pelts and tobacco, to buy cheaply and then sell for large profits back home.

At first, these visitors were tolerated by the American Indians. They were even welcomed because they brought useful items that the native people didn't have. The Wampanoag and their neighbors were pleased to trade plentiful beaver pelts for finely made metal objects such as knives, hatchets, iron kettles, and especially guns. The American Indians realized that with guns, they could obtain more beaver pelts. They could then trade the pelts to the Europeans for more guns and other

American Indians on the northeastern coast traded beaver pelts for other goods, such as guns, with the Europeans. The Wampanoag soon realized that guns would help protect them from some of their neighbors.

European trade goods. The white men, for their part, were just as pleased. Beaver skin hats were a popular fashion in Europe, and so beaver pelts were in great demand and could be sold for a high price.

The American Indians came to realize that guns provided another advantage. A small, relatively weak tribe could more easily defend itself against invasion if it had guns. A tribe that was already large and powerful could more easily attack weaker tribes if it had guns. Because of European guns, the balance of power between the Wampanoag and the Narragansett would eventually shift.

Waves of Disease

The European visitors unknowingly brought something else with them to North America. Unexplained illnesses began to affect the native people. Without realizing it, the explorers and traders carried European diseases to North America, such as smallpox, measles, chicken pox, influenza, and bubonic plague. These diseases had existed for hundreds of years in Europe, and periodically killed large numbers of people there. But over the years, many Europeans developed **immunity** to these diseases. This meant that they could become ill from the germs but recover, or carry the germs in their bodies without becoming sick. However, they could still spread the germs to other people, usually without even knowing it.

These germs had never existed in North America. The American Indians had no immunity from them. As a result,

An illustration depicts members of a Wampanoag community dying from smallpox.

once Europeans brought the germs to North America, huge numbers of the American Indian population became ill and died in **epidemics**. Every few years a European brought a new germ or a germ was carried from one American Indian community to another. Each time, a new epidemic broke out.

In about 1619, one particularly devastating epidemic hit the Wampanoag. A great plague (probably measles) killed

How Many?

No one knows for sure how many American Indians lived in southern New England before European settlement began. Estimates range from eight thousand to twelve thousand before the epidemics, but only about two to five thousand by 1620.

most of the Wampanoag living on the mainland. Many villages were wiped out completely. By the time the epidemic subsided, more than half of the Wampanoag population had died.

The year 1620 was one of grief for the Wampanoag. Their sachem, Massasoit, believed that his people had somehow angered the spirits. They had to find a way to **appease** them. In addition, the Wampanoag faced new troubles from the Narragansett, who were spared from the epidemic by their distance across the large bay. The Narragansett were again eyeing Wampanoag lands. For the first time, Massasoit's people were vastly outnumbered by their enemies to the west. If the Narragansett attacked, the Wampanoag would not be strong enough to hold them off.

A New Kind of Visitor

In December 1620, a European ship arrived and docked at Patuxet, a Wampanoag village that had been wiped out by the epidemic. Aboard the ship were not explorers or traders who would do business and then leave, but settlers. They were families with children, looking for a place to live. These families were English. They were known as Pilgrims, and their ship was the *Mayflower*.

The Pilgrims saw signs of habitation everywhere around Patuxet, but they found no people. A village of wetus sat empty. There were fields for planting, but no one tended them. It appeared to them that God had prepared this place

The arrival of the Pilgrims would change the lives of the Wampanoag forever.

especially for them. William Bradford, a leader of the settlers, declared that there was "none to hinder our possession or to lay claim to it." It wasn't God, however, but disease that had left the village empty.

The English settlers began to cut trees and build English-style houses at Patuxet. They called their settlement Plymouth. It was winter, however, and the Pilgrims had nothing to eat except what they had brought with them on the *Mayflower*. They foraged for food as best they could. Sometimes had to resort to stealing corn from Wampanoag graves. That first winter, half of the 102 English settlers died.

Unexpected Winter

Plymouth was at the same **latitude** as Spain, and so the Pilgrims had expected a warm country with mild winters. But the winter in this place was even colder than it had been in England.

During the winter, Massasoit and his counselors observed the settlers from a distance. They could see that they were starving. They could also see that they intended to stay. If these settlers were going to survive another winter, they would need help.

The Wampanoag needed help too. The few that were left after the epidemic were being **harassed** by the powerful Narragansett. If the Wampanoag became allies of these English settlers with guns, the Narragansett might leave them alone.

Perhaps Massasoit also thought that helping the strangers would please the angered spirits. In addition, since he lived by

The Pilgrims had not prepared for a difficult winter. They thought that their new home would be warmer than it was.

the principles of reciprocity, he was obligated to share what he had with others. But more than that, Massasoit knew how hard it was to see your people die in such great numbers. He had earned the role of sachem because he was a wise and compassionate leader. He proved this again when he decided to help the Pilgrims.

A Treaty and a Feast

In March of 1621, Massasoit sent two representatives to the settlers. They were Samoset, an Abenaki Indian who had learned some English from traders, and Tisquantum (Squanto). Tisquantum was a Wampanoag who had once been kidnapped by traders and had spent several years in Europe. Samoset astounded the white settlers with the words, "Hello, Englishmen."

Soon afterward, Massasoit himself met with John Carver, the governor of Plymouth Colony. Together they drew up a **treaty**. They each promised to let the other group live in peace and to defend each other against enemies.

A few weeks later, when Governor Carver died unexpectedly, William Bradford was elected governor of Plymouth Colony. He reaffirmed the treaty that had been signed with Massasoit. Bradford would remain a leader of the colony and a friend of Massasoit for many years. Both men would honor this treaty for as long as they lived.

During the summer of 1621, Massasoit's people showed

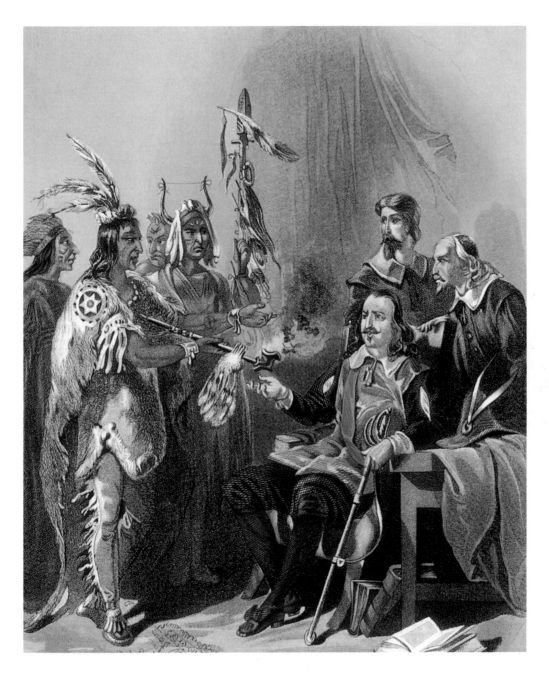

*Massasoit and John Carver negotiated a treaty between the Wampanoag and the
Pilgrims, which was intended to help both groups survive.*

While the Wampanoag and the Pilgrims did share a meal on the "First Thanksgiving," this painting may not be the most accurate depiction of the day's events. For example, probably only Wampanoag men attended.

the Pilgrims how to grow corn and beans. They showed them where to fish and hunt.

By the autumn of the year, the Pilgrims had a small but suitable harvest. This time, they were ready for winter. They invited Massasoit to join them for a celebration. He accepted the invitation, and brought ninety men with him.

For three days, the two communities feasted and played games together. This harvest celebration, so similar to the traditional celebration observed by the Wampanoag for generations, is what we commemorate today as the "First Thanksgiving."

The tiny community of Pilgrims survived with the help of Massasoit and his people. Pilgrim men and firearms provided the Wampanoag with additional defenses against the Narragansett. Massasoit's friendship was protection for the Pilgrims as well, who lived in constant fear of attack from unknown tribes. It was truly a relationship of reciprocity.

In the years to follow, however, Massasoit's descendants would come to regret the help their people gave to these first European settlers. The **migration** started as a trickle, with just a handful of English people moving to North America. But that trickle would soon become a flood.

More and more ships arrived after the **Mayflower,** *bringing* **English people interested in settling in North America.**

Chapter Three

The European Invasion

In the years following the arrival of the Pilgrims, the European migration grew, and then exploded. In November of 1621, a second group of Pilgrims arrived to join those at Plymouth. In 1628, five more ships arrived, carrying two hundred English to this region, which had become known as "New England." They settled north of Plymouth on Massachusetts Bay, naming their town Salem and establishing the Massachusetts Bay Colony. In 1630, one thousand more

Move Over, Neighbor

Just three weeks after the 1621 harvest celebration, a ship called the *Fortune* arrived from England with thirty-five passengers, ready to settle at Plymouth. The *Mayflower* settlers had just struggled through a difficult year and had finally harvested enough to feed themselves. Now, just as another difficult winter was approaching, they had thirty-five additional mouths to feed.

English settlers arrived. By 1634, the Massachusetts Bay Colony had grown to four thousand. By 1638, the population was eleven thousand. By 1643, there were twenty thousand English settlers living in Massachusetts.

The settlers brought cows and sheep with them from England. They continued to build houses, and their villages grew larger. They built fences to keep in their animals. They established new villages farther and farther inland.

In the short span of twenty-two years, the population of European settlers blossomed from zero to twenty thousand people. This wave of settlers has become known as the Great Migration. It must have seemed more like an invasion to the Wampanoag people, who had only recently seen their own population nearly wiped out by foreign disease.

A Difference of Opinion

As the English population grew, its leaders kept returning to Massasoit and the sachems of the other tribes. They wanted to buy land. Their homeland of England was a small, densely populated island, and owning land was an **unattainable** luxury

Birth of Boston

The settlers arriving in 1630 established a settlement of their own just south of Salem, naming it after their hometown in England. Thus, Boston, Massachusetts, was born.

for most people. Only the nobility or the very rich owned land, passing it down from one generation to the next. Here in the New World, land stretched on seemingly forever, virtually empty and (in the minds of the settlers) waiting for someone to claim it. For the first time in their lives, these settlers had the opportunity to be landowners.

The Wampanoag were perplexed by these white settlers who wanted to own land. To the Wampanoag, land could not be bought and sold any more than the air could be bought and sold. Besides, these lands were vital to the survival of the

The way of life for the Wampanoag was threatened by the growing English population. The English wanted to own some of the land that the Wampanoag used for hunting and fishing.

"Praying Towns"

The English, so sure that their Puritan religion was the proper religion, set out to convert as many American Indians as they could. They established "praying towns," where Christianized Indians would live. They would learn to read and write in English, dress like the English, and hear the Gospel. By 1675, there were fourteen "praying towns" in New England, with more than a thousand "praying Indians." However, most "praying Indians" continued to practice their "pagan" ways in addition to being good Christians. They hunted and fished on Sundays, and they continued to conduct traditional rituals honoring the old spirits. Thus, they were never fully accepted in white society. At the same time, their own people sometimes distrusted them for adopting English ways.

Wampanoag. They were hunting grounds, fishing grounds, and ancient trails connecting the two. The Wampanoag needed to be able to use these lands in the same way they always had. They needed to maintain their way of life, feed their families, and prosper once more.

Massasoit knew that the English also needed land to plant their crops and feed their families. And the Wampanoag continued to benefit from good relations with the English. They still received protection from the Narragansett. They could obtain the European-made axes, cookware, firearms, and woolen clothing that had become necessities. In addition, it was a sad fact that the Wampanoag needed less land than before, since their numbers had been so greatly diminished by disease. Therefore, while Massasoit could not sell the land to the white settlers, he was willing to share it. He, and sachems of other tribes as well, signed new treaties entitling the Europeans to use more and more tracts of land. Each year, the European settlements extended closer to the remaining Wampanoag villages.

Prosperity and Growth

As the English population grew during the years of the Great Migration, so did that of the Wampanoag, although much more slowly. The waves of disease had subsided and Massasoit's people enjoyed health and prosperity. Their original kindness to the settlers of Plymouth Colony was being repaid in good relations and good trade. There was still plenty of land

Rhode Island

Rhode Island was not invited to join the United Colonies alliance. Established in 1636 by Roger Williams as a refuge for Quakers and other non-conforming religious groups, it was looked upon by the other colonists as a society of outcasts.

for everyone. Any disputes were quickly settled by Massasoit and the leaders of Plymouth Colony, including William Bradford, who had known and respected Massasoit for many years. In 1639, to demonstrate the continued **solidarity** of the two communities, Massasoit and Bradford officially reaffirmed the "ancient treaty" they had signed in 1621.

Soon thereafter, however, a new alliance was formed. In 1643, the colonies of Massachusetts, Plymouth, New Haven, and Connecticut formed an alliance called the United Colonies. Instead of looking to the Wampanoag or other Indians for protection and support, the English colonists began to look to each other.

A New Generation

In 1657, Massasoit's old friend William Bradford died. Four years later, in 1661, Massasoit himself died, passing the title of sachem to his eldest son, Wamsutta. The signers of the original treaty were gone and a new generation now took their place. This generation had no memory of the beginning of the colony. They didn't remember the days when colonists were only a handful of starving newcomers, and the Wampanoag

were a nearly extinct people at the mercy of more powerful tribes.

The English population continued to grow. By the time of Massasoit's death, there were more than thirty thousand Europeans living in the southern New England colonies of Massachusetts, Plymouth, Rhode Island, New Haven, and Connecticut. Each year, new towns were established farther and farther inland. By about 1670, only fifty years after the *Mayflower* had arrived, the white population outnumbered the American Indian population in southern New England.

Relations between the English and the Wampanoag were different now. The trust and support the two communities had shared and provided in the past began to erode. The colonists far outnumbered the Wampanoag. They no longer needed them for protection or survival. They began to look at the Wampanoag, and other tribes, as an obstacle to the further colonization of New England.

Stubbornly Independent

Plymouth Colony remained a separate colony until 1692, when it became part of Massachusetts Colony.

Metacom helped his brother Wamsutta and traveled with him to meet with the English.

Chapter Four

King Philip's War

Wamsutta was well aware that his people were now at a disadvantage. He wanted to preserve what was left of Wampanoag lands. But he also knew he would have to keep peace with the colonists. Soon after he became sachem, Wamsutta and his younger brother, Metacom, traveled to Plymouth to meet with the English authorities. To show that he respected both cultures equally, he accepted English names for himself and his brother.

Thereafter, Wamsutta was called Alexander by the colonists. Metacom was called Philip.

Despite this gesture, mistrust between the two cultures grew. With no personal friendships between the colonists and the Wampanoag, suspicions grew on both sides. Rumors spread among the colonists that one tribe or another was planning an uprising. Wamsutta, who felt no particular allegiance to the Plymouth colonists, negotiated a land deal with Rhode Island. When the Plymouth authorities heard about this deal, they sent for Wamsutta.

Wamsutta refused to go to Plymouth. In response, Josiah Winslow, a major in the colonial **militia** and son of Governor Edward Winslow, marched out with a company of armed guards to get Wamsutta and bring him before the Plymouth authorities.

Whether by consent or by force, Wamsutta traveled with Winslow to Plymouth. He met with the officials, but then he fell ill. He stayed at Winslow's home, where an English doctor

treated him, but he did not improve. Wamsutta decided to make the journey back home anyway. He died on the way.

Wamsutta's sudden death alarmed and angered the Wampanoag. Some of them, including his brother Metacom, suspected that he was poisoned, but the English denied the accusation. In this atmosphere of mistrust, Metacom became sachem of the Wampanoag.

The Wampanoag found the death of Wamsutta mysterious and it added to their distrust of the English.

"King Philip"

Metacom, now called "King Philip" by the colonists, was even less trusting than his brother. He had spent his life watching the white settlers multiply and take even more land. His

A Harvard Man

John Sassamon was the first American Indian to attend Harvard College. It was established in 1636 by the Massachusetts Bay Colony, and is the oldest institution of higher learning in the United States. It became Harvard University in 1780.

father's compassion and generosity toward a desperate handful of settlers forty years earlier had turned out to be the first drop of a tidal wave that now threatened to drown out Metacom's own people. If settlement continued to spread as it had, there would be no place left for the Wampanoag to live.

Metacom began to consult with his advisors. One of these men was John Sassamon, a "praying Indian" who had been educated at Harvard College. When Metacom became sachem, Sassamon returned to the Wampanoag.

Metacom realized that his own people could not resist the white settlers on their own. Other tribes were experiencing the same **encroachment** of their lands. If Metacom could arrange alliances with those other tribes, together they might be able to turn back the tide of European settlement.

An alliance between tribes was not easily formed, however. The long tradition of **animosity** between tribes such as the Wampanoag and Narragansett would be hard to put aside, even now, when they had a common goal.

With tribal alliances in question, Metacom spent several years trying diplomatic ways of working out differences with the English. He met with colonial authorities when they asked him to. He appeared in their courts to dispute land claims. Still, the colonists continued to press for more land. They asked Metacom to sign treaties subjecting himself and his people to their authority.

Metacom's advisors pressed him to stand up to the English. The Wampanoag wanted to stop giving up their land. Some of them pushed for the tribal alliances. But Metacom was determined to work out a peaceful solution.

Rumors of American Indian unrest began to trickle to Plymouth and to Boston. In 1671, authorities from Plymouth and Massachusetts Bay colonies insisted that Metacom turn over all of the Wampanoag's weapons. Even if he wanted to cooperate, Metacom knew that the men of his tribe were not about to give up all their firearms. He did not agree to turn over the weapons.

This tense **diplomacy** continued for several more years. All the while, Metacom continued to try to build alliances with the other tribes.

The Spark

Then, in January 1675, John Sassamon unexpectedly left Metacom's circle of advisors. Perhaps they had a disagreement. Perhaps Metacom suspected Sassamon of informing the English. In any case, Sassamon left the Wampanoag village and returned to live among the colonists.

Soon afterward, Sassamon was found drowned under the ice of a pond. Three Wampanoag men were accused of murder by the Plymouth authorities and put on trial.

Despite their pleas of innocence, and despite the presence of American Indians on the jury, the men were found guilty of the murder and hanged. More than ever, both English and Wampanoag expected war.

The Flame

A colonial representative from Rhode Island made a desperate attempt to negotiate with Metacom. He offered to appoint two **arbitrators**, or impartial judges, to hear Metacom's grievances and find a solution. The arbitrators would be a colonial governor and an American Indian sachem.

Metacom said that he would consider arbitration, but he

still had a major grievance. His father Massasoit had fed and protected the English when they were helpless. Now their positions were reversed. The English were powerful and Metacom's people were weak. Yet the English were not acting toward the Wampanoag as Massasoit had acted toward the English. In other words, the colonists had failed to honor the principle of reciprocity.

The proposed arbitration never took place. Shortly thereafter, on June 20, 1675, a band of Wampanoag, perhaps unknown to Metacom, attacked the English settlement of Swansea. King Philip's War had begun.

War broke out after the promised discussion to address Metacom's concerns never materialized.

Choosing Sides

It was not a conventional war. Neither the American Indians nor the English had an organized army. Neither side had much of a plan. It was more accurately an increasingly deadly series of raids and counter-raids of both native and English villages.

It was not even strictly American Indians against the colonists. Some tribes, like the Wampanoag at the tip of Cape Cod, chose to stay out of the war completely. Some, like the Mohegan in Connecticut, sided with the English. Some, like the Narragansett, refused to fight on either side, but took in Wampanoag women and children when they were driven from their homes.

Even the alliance between English colonies was shaky, as militias from the different colonies argued among themselves over supplies and strategy. Each side, however, did have one major goal. Metacom's goal was to drive all the English back to the coast. The colonists' goal was to capture and destroy Metacom.

A Brutal War

Although they were far outnumbered, Metacom's armies were very familiar with the terrain. They used their ancient hunting trails to evade the English and join with fighting men from other tribes. They raided village after village, setting buildings on fire and killing men, women, and children.

The English armies were just as brutal. They attacked Indian villages without mercy, burning them to the ground. No village or family, whether colonist or Indian, felt safe during that savage year.

By August 1676, more than half of the ninety English settlements in southern New England had been torched. Most of the colonists had fled to coastal cities for protection. Metacom was coming very close to achieving his goal of driving the English back to the coast.

Then, in that same month, a group of English soldiers received word from a Wampanoag informant that Metacom was camped in a swamp near Mount Hope, Rhode Island. The English soldiers marched to the swamp, surrounded Metacom, and shot him.

News of Metacom's death spread quickly among both the English and the American Indians. Far outnumbered and now without a leader, the

The English located Metacom and killed him. Without his leadership, the Indian forces lost their will to continue the fight.

American Indian forces fell apart, fled, or surrendered. In the same fractured way that it had been fought, the war had come to an end.

The Cost of War

Southern New England lay in ruin. Fifty-two English villages, and uncounted native villages, had been partially or totally destroyed.

The cost in lives was even more devastating. Eight hundred English died in the war. More than three thousand American

King Philip's War is considered to be the deadliest war fought in America.

Indians were killed, or 15 percent of the entire native population of New England. In proportion to population, King Philip's War had been, and still is, the deadliest American war ever fought.

Aftermath and Dispersal

The American Indians who survived lost virtually everything. Many were sold into slavery. Many fled west or north to find refuge with other tribes.

Of the mainland Wampanoag, only about four hundred survived. Those who remained were allowed to live in or near Mashpee, a "praying town" on Cape Cod, where they were forced to live under English rule.

Metacom's hopes for regaining his homeland had failed. The Wampanoag people had shown mercy and compassion toward the first English settlers less than sixty years earlier. Now they had been swept aside and nearly wiped out by the flood of European settlers who followed.

Despite the disastrous losses in King Philip's War, the Wampanoag and their culture continues to this day. Here, a group of Wampanoag perform during a powwaw.

Chapter Five

The Wampanoag Today

American Indian culture had dominated New England for thousands of years until the 1600s. King Philip's War marked the decisive end of that domination. The war assured the white settlement of New England without native interference.

The small Wampanoag settlements at Mashpee and at Gay Head on the island of Martha's Vineyard remained after the war. They are the two centers of Wampanoag culture today, with a combined population of about three thousand.

Quest for Federal Recognition

In recent years, the Wampanoag people have been trying to achieve federal recognition as American Indian tribes. Federal recognition is a legal relationship with the Unites States government. It allows a tribe to claim specific lands for its own use. The tribe can establish some of its own laws and government within those lands. This is particularly important to the Wampanoag tribe. Their homelands on Cape Cod and Martha's Vineyard are near heavily populated beach resorts.

While honoring the past, the Wampanoag work to build their future. A group of Mashpee Wampanoag elders pose for a photograph. They are still working for federal recognition for their people.

The Wampanoag have had to fight to keep these lands from overdevelopment in recent years.

The two largest Wampanoag communities have applied for federal recognition. The Aquinnah (Gay Head) Wampanoag of Martha's Vineyard were awarded recognition in 1987. They have established a cultural center and a library to preserve Wampanoag history and traditions.

The Mashpee Wampanoag of Cape Cod have been requesting recognition since 1976. They are still waiting for a decision from the U.S. government. In 2004, a bill was introduced in the House of Representatives, again requesting recognition for the Mashpee Wampanoag. Federal recognition would allow the Mashpee to buy back some traditional tribal lands and preserve them from development.

Preserving an Ancient Culture

It is important to the Wampanoag to preserve their cultural heritage and teach it to their children. The Wampanoag language, once outlawed, has been revived and is being taught to tribal members. As in ancient times, members of each Wampanoag community work together to take care of their poor and elderly members. The traditional

This sculpture depicts one of the recent chiefs of the Mashpee Wampanoag.

A Mashpee Wampanoag mother and child dress in traditional clothing.

positions of sachem and holy man are still recognized by each Wampanoag community. The powwaw ceremony was revived in the twentieth century. It is held every year in the town of Mashpee, Massachusetts.

For more than four hundred years, the Wampanoag have lived in the shadow of a culture much different from their own. They signed the white people's treaties, accepted their Christian God as equal to their own spirits, and even agreed to be called by English names. Today, the Wampanoag are active members of two cultures. As they work to revive their native heritage, they also embrace their role as American citizens. They live, work, and go to school side by side with Americans of all races. In honor of this dual heritage, the Mashpee powwaw ceremony is held every year on the Fourth of July.

The Wampanoag heritage is a vital piece of American history. They are the People of the First Light. They are the people who first welcomed strangers to their lands. Massasoit's sons came to regret the results of their father's hospitality. But

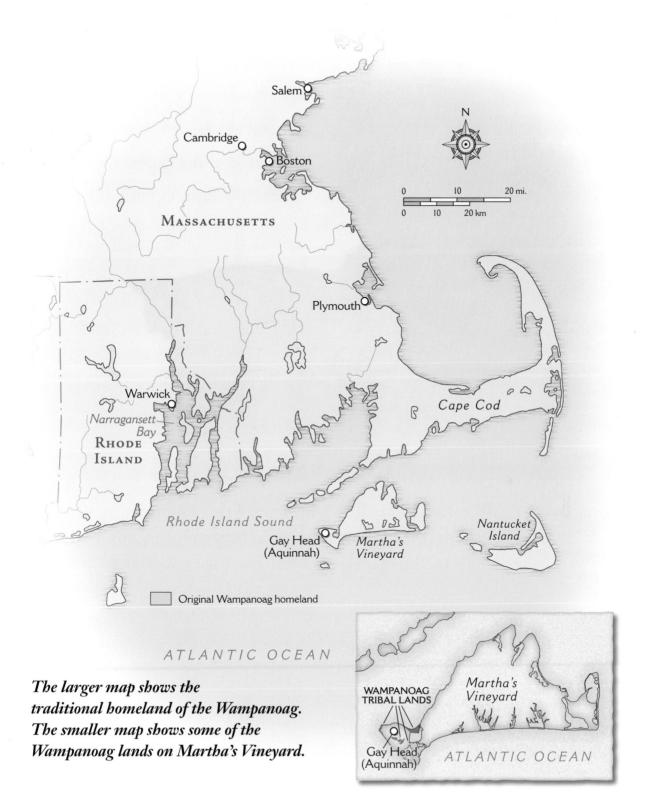

Salem

Cambridge

Boston

MASSACHUSETTS

N

0   10   20 mi.

0   10   20 km

Plymouth

Cape Cod

Warwick

Narragansett Bay

RHODE ISLAND

Rhode Island Sound

Gay Head (Aquinnah)

Martha's Vineyard

Nantucket Island

Original Wampanoag homeland

ATLANTIC OCEAN

The larger map shows the traditional homeland of the Wampanoag. The smaller map shows some of the Wampanoag lands on Martha's Vineyard.

WAMPANOAG TRIBAL LANDS

Martha's Vineyard

Gay Head (Aquinnah)

ATLANTIC OCEAN

Young Wampanoag children learn about their heritage by participating in a powwaw.

Massasoit himself would never have doubted that showing generosity and compassion to hungry strangers was his proper duty to the spirits who had been so generous to his own people.

Modern-Day Powwaw

The first Wampanoag powwaw after King Philip's War was held in 1918, over two hundred years later.

Timeline

1524	Giovanni da Verrazano explores the North American coast for France, including Narragansett Bay, in the homeland of the Wampanoag.
1617–1619	Epidemics spread among the Wampanoag, killing more than half of the population.
1620	The English ship *Mayflower* arrives, bringing the first European settlers to New England.
1621	In March, Massasoit and Governor John Carver sign a treaty between the Wampanoag and the Plymouth settlers. In October, the Pilgrims invite the Wampanoag to share in a three-day harvest feast (the "First Thanksgiving").
1630–1643	The "Great Migration" of English colonists occurs, with 20,000 settlers living in New England by 1643, only twenty-two years after the first settlers arrived.
1661	Massasoit dies. His son Wamsutta (Alexander) becomes sachem of the Wampanoag.
1662	Wamsutta dies mysteriously while returning from a meeting at Plymouth; his brother Metacom (Philip) becomes sachem.
1663	About 30,000 European colonists now live in southern New England.
1675–1676	King Philip's War takes place.
1676–1678	Dispersal of Wampanoag survivors to slavery and "praying towns."

1700s	"Praying towns" of Mashpee and Gay Head become centers of Wampanoag population.
1976	The Mashpee Wampanoag request official recognition from the federal government.
1987	The Aquinnah (Gay Head) Wampanoag are granted official tribal recognition from the United States government.

Glossary

animosity—ill will, hostility

appease—to bring to a state of peace or quiet

arbitrator—a person appointed to impartially settle a dispute

diplomacy—the practice of discussion and negotiation between two nations

dispersal—the process of sending out or spreading

encroachment—advancing beyond normal limits, intrusion

epidemic—a disease spreading quickly and affecting many people

exclusive—limited, excluding use by others

harass—to cause trouble repeatedly

immunity—the ability to resist a certain disease

latitude—a distance measured north or south of the equator

migration—the movement of people from one place to another

militia—a group of citizens organized as an army

powwaw—a Wampanoag holy person or spiritual leader. A ceremonial gathering.

reciprocity—an equal exchange of trade or of courtesies between two people or societies

sachem—a Wampanoag community leader who usually acts with consent from advisors

solidarity—union or agreement between groups

treaty—a written agreement between two nations or groups

unattainable—not able to be obtained or possessed

wetu—a circular or oval Wampanoag dwelling made of saplings bent together and covered with mats of woven grass or animal skins

To Find Out More

Books

Collier, Christopher, and James Lincoln Collier. *Clash of Cultures: Prehistory to 1638*. New York: Marshall Cavendish, 1998.

Collier, Christopher, and James Lincoln Collier. *Pilgrims and Puritans: 1620–1676*. New York: Marshall Cavendish, 1998.

Grace, Catherine O'Neill, et al. *1621: A New Look at Thanksgiving*. Washington, D.C.: National Geographic, 2001.

Josephy, Alvin. *500 Nations: An Illustrated History of North American Indians*. New York: Gramercy Press, 2002.

Peters, Russell M. *Clambake: A Wampanoag Tradition (We Are Still Here)*. Minneapolis: Lerner Publishing, 1992.

Organizations and Online Sites

i-Boston: Your Guide to Massachusetts History
http://www.iboston.org
This site offers a funny but insightful explanation of how New England came to be settled by English separatists, from their quarrels with the English king to their establishment of the city of Boston.

The Mashantucket Pequot Museum and Research Center
http://www.pequotmuseum.org
A living history museum explains on its Web site the history and culture of the Pequot tribe, neighbors of the Wampanoag and participants in King Philip's War.

Plimoth Plantation
http://www.plimoth.org
This very informative site explains how the Wampanoag and Pilgrims lived in the 1620s, with many fascinating details.

The Wampanoag: People of the First Light
http://www.bostonkids.org/educators/wampanoag.html#
This informative site is sponsored by the Boston Children's Museum and contains photos, links, and activities.

The Wampanoag Tribe of Gay Head (Aquinnah)
http://www.wampanoagtribe.net
This site describes the history of the Wampanoag on the island of Martha's Vineyard and their community today.

A Note on Sources

One of the most interesting parts of doing research for *The Wampanoag* was how much the opinions of scholars have changed over the years. You can still read books that depict American Indians as "savages" and the English colonists as God's chosen people in the New World.

Later books tend to reverse that outlook completely, and to the other extreme: American Indians were "noble" and had a perfect society, and the colonists were thieves who tricked the native people out of their lands.

The most recent books are finally searching for a middle ground, respecting both the American Indian and European cultures, and trying to understand the good qualities and the faults of both groups. The two books that did the best job in this regard were *Clash of Cultures: Prehistory to 1638* by Christopher and James Collier, and *King Philip's War: The*

History and Legacy of America's Forgotten Conflict by Eric Schultz and Michael Tougias.

My goal was to present the same sort of balanced, respectful interpretation in this book.

—*Stacy DeKeyser*

Index

Numbers in *italics* indicate illustrations.

About the Author

Stacy DeKeyser lives in Simsbury, Connecticut, which happens to be one of the English colonial towns that was burned to the ground during King Philip's War. She has hiked part of the Metacom Trail nearby, which is still heavily wooded and, according to local legend, was used by Metacom and his fighting men during the war. She has heard rumors of a hiding place along the trail called King Philip's Cave, but she hasn't found it yet.

She is a graduate of UCLA and Arizona State University.